WORD PLAY

COLOR WORDS

green

yellow

by Carrie B. Sheely

PEBBLE

a capstone imprint

Red **and** orange.
Yellow **and** green.

Look at a rainbow. You'll see these colors and more. Find out what other colors are around!

red **orange** yellow

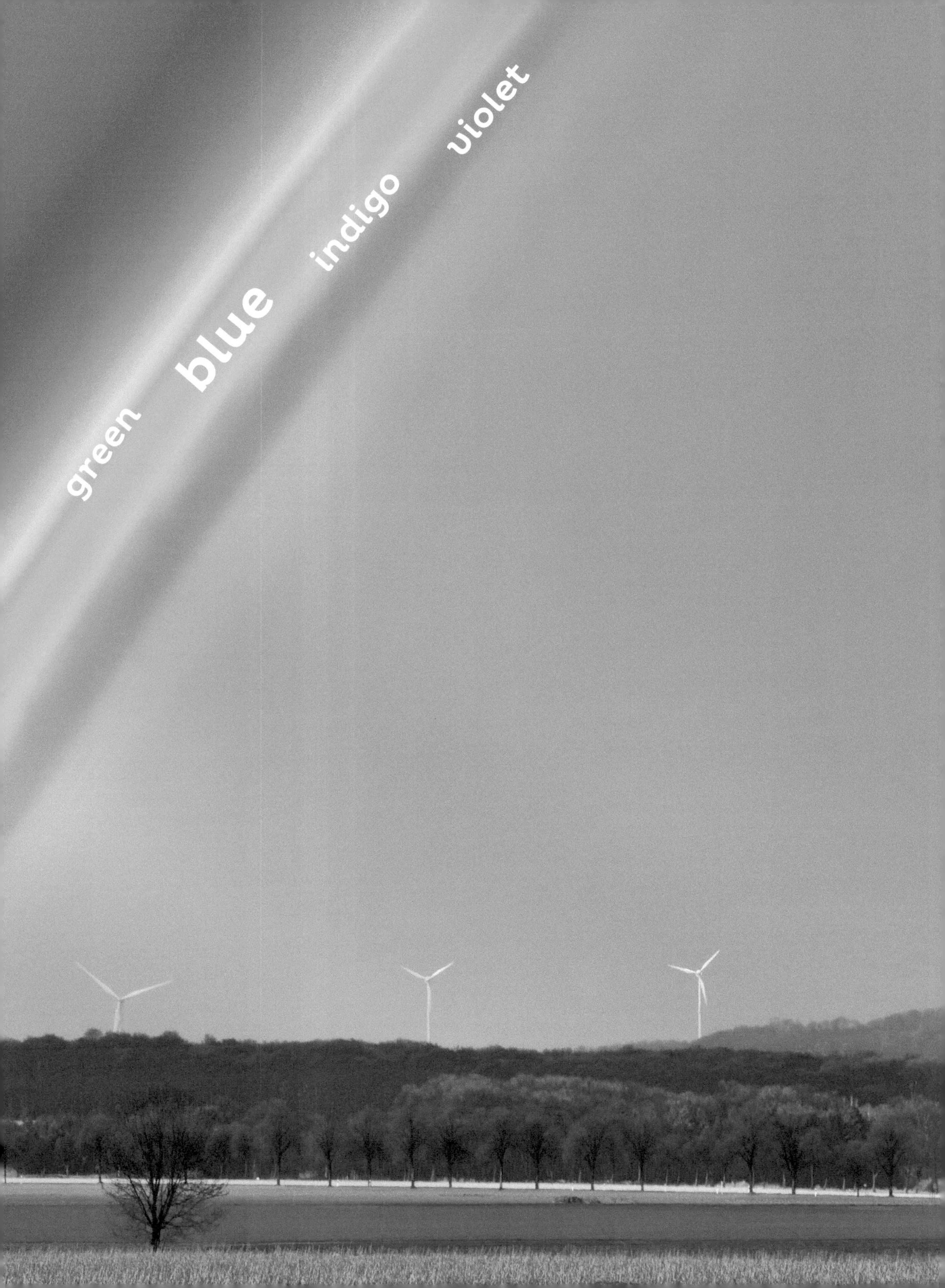
green
blue
indigo
violet

orange

coral

rust

goldenrod

yellow

yellow

yellow

emerald

olive

green

green

green

lime

green

azure

navy

indigo

violet

lavender

beige

cinnamon

tan

fawn

brown

red

crimson

burgundy

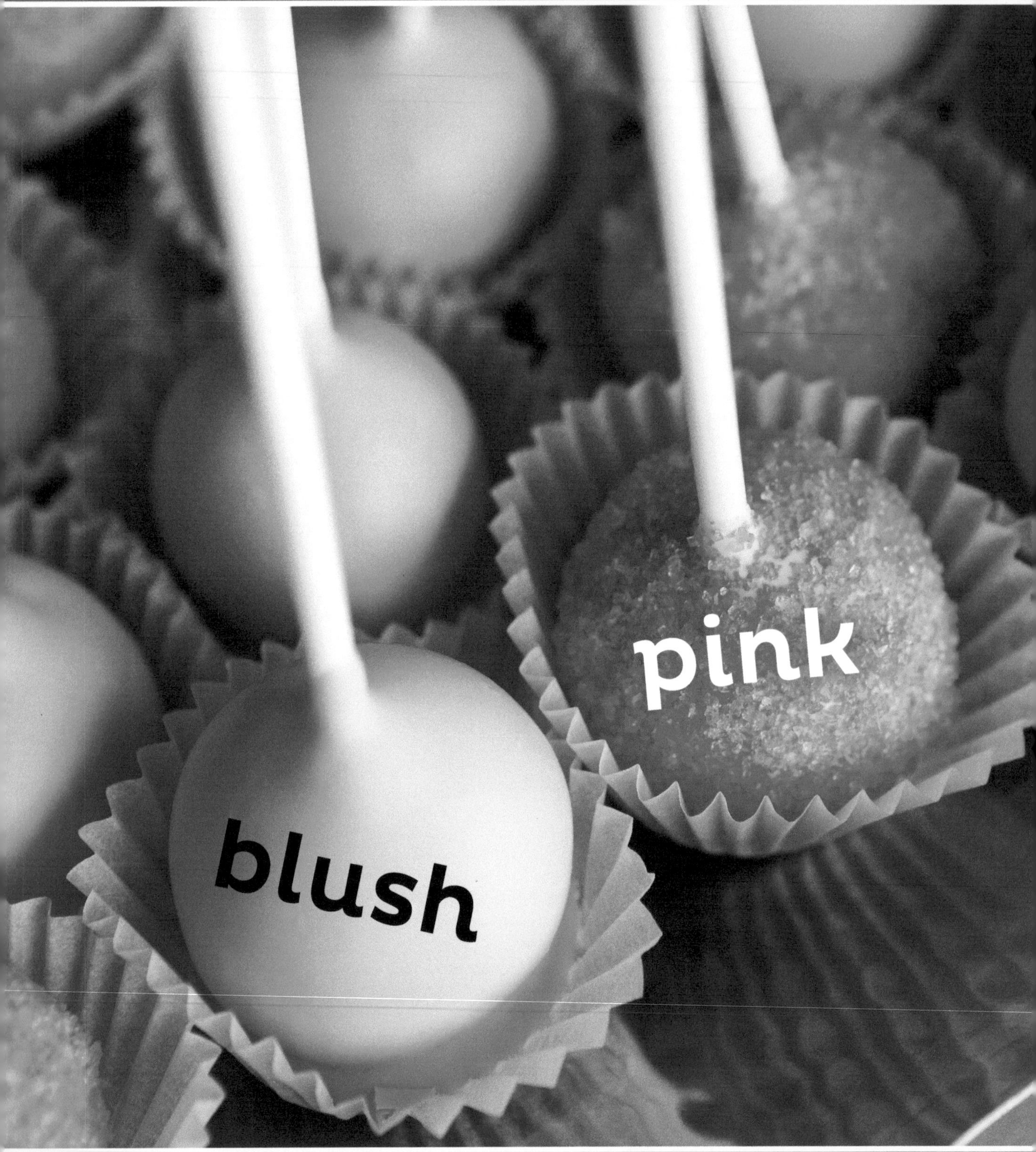
pink
blush

fuchsia

What other color words do you see?

orchid

purple

periwinkle

white

black

turquoise

cyan

teal

cream

taupe

gold

Pebble Sprout is published by Pebble,
an imprint of Capstone.
1710 Roe Crest Drive
North Mankato, Minnesota 56003
www.capstonepub.com

**Library of Congress Cataloging-in-Publication Data
is available on the Library of Congress website.**
ISBN: 978-1-9771-2365-7 (library binding)
ISBN: 978-1-9771-2366-4 (paperback)
ISBN: 978-1-9771-2367-1 (eBook PDF)

Summary: Through engaging photos,
introduces colors.

Image Credits
Dreamstime: Badunchik, 14 (bottom); iStockphoto: 27 (top),
Image Source, 4; Shutterstock: Anastacia Petrova, 18–19
(bottom), Beautiful landscape, 12, Bernie Van Der Vyver, 17,
Billy Gadbury, 18 (top), cahya nugraha, 27 (bottom), Cheryl
Casey, 21, covenant, 24, Darren Green, 7 (top), denizya, 1,
Dmitry Tsvetkov, 10–11, Ekaterina Kuzovkova, 22 (bottom),
Glenn Price, 16 (bottom), Guas, 30–31, HTeam, 28–29, John
L. Absher, 13, Kasefoto, 26, M. Relova, 14–15, Margarita
Borodina, 2–3, Mountains Hunter, 23, Niti Tangpaitoon,
25, Patrick Reith, 16 (top), Peter_ml, 9, PhotographyByMK,
7 (bottom), Prostock-studio, 20, Richard Whitcombe, 5,
Scarc, 22 (top), Simon Shim, 8 (top), Susanne Fritzsche, 6,
Tetyana Kaganska, 19 (top), topseller, cover, Zapfl Cornelia,
8 (bottom)

Editorial Credits
Designer: Juliette Peters
Media Researcher: Svetlana Zhurkin
Production Specialist: Katy LaVigne

Titles in this set:

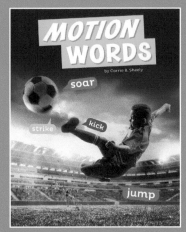

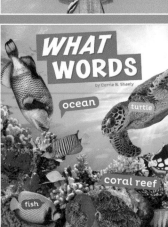

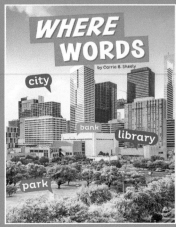